There is some timeless thread which binds us to this place.
It must be more than colors, songs and half-remembered names!
When first I walked the Oval, frightened, homesick, unprepared;
It seemed it all began that day...that not a soul had been this way before.
My era scoffed at tales of glory past; Ohio Field and other ancient lore.

Then, when my June came, and put the miles between town and gown,
I thought the books were closed—in fact—and in the audit sense.
Instead I found myself in groups whose primal bond was Alma Mater shared;
Where age and college year became statistics laughed away...
Our common niche 15th and High, when failure never faintly loomed.

Milton Caniff, in " Now In My Day "

*The function of a university is not to teach the means of life only,
but life itself; not only how to make a living, but how to live.*

Joseph R. Taylor, in *The Ohio State University Quarterly*,
October, 1911

THE
OHIO STATE
UNIVERSITY

PHOTOGRAPHED BY BARTH FALKENBERG

HARMONY HOUSE
Publishers Louisville

The making of *The Ohio State University* was a cooperative effort, and a most pleasant and professional one at that. We are indebted to many people at the University who made our job easier, and who share in the production credits. From the Alumni Association are : Dan L. Heinlen, Director of Alumni Affairs ; Ron D. Hopper, Associate Director ; and Linda S. Crossley, Communications Director. From University Communications are : Malcolm Baroway, Executive Director ; David Hoover, Director of University Publications ; and University Photographers J. Kevin Fitzsimons and Lloyd Lemmermann. From the University are : John T. Mount, Vice-President and Dean Emeritus ; Bertha Ihnat, University Archives Assistant for Manuscripts ; and Ruth Jones, University Archives Assistant for Photographs.

Mr. Fitzsimons' photographs appear on pages 30, 49, 59 and 101.
Mr. Lemmermann's photographs appear on pages 25, 92, and 109.
Their photographs are used with the permission of The
Ohio State University.

Executive Editors: William Butler and William Strode
Library of Congress Catalog Number: 86-082730
Hardcover International Standard Book Number 0-916509-08-7
Printed in USA by Pinaire Lithographing Corp., Louisville, Kentucky
Edition printed February, 1987 by Harmony House Publishers,
P.O.Box 90, Prospect, Kentucky 40059   (502) 228-2010 / 228-4446
Copyright © 1987 by Harmony House Publishers
Photographs copyright © Barth Falkenberg

Orton Hall

University Hall

A SONG TO ALMA MATER RAISED

This book is a tribute to The Ohio University, the Alma Mater I share with more than 250,000 other alumni. It is not an attempt to catalog this college or that, but instead it is a look at the essence of the University.

Founded in 1870 as part of the federal land grant program for higher education, Ohio State was pledged to have as its leading object the teaching of such branches of learning "as are related to agriculture and mechanical arts, in such a manner as the legislatures of the states may repectively prescribe, in order to promote the liberal and practical education of the industrial classes in the several pursuits and professions of life," according to the legislation. After more than a century of the very finest teaching, research, and public service, Ohio State is a world-class institution poised for a position of pre-eminence in the twenty-first century.

The knowledge that can be found at Ohio State is virtually limitless. The organization to impart and pursue that knowledge means 19 colleges, seven schools, and a graduate school; some 229 undergraduate majors and 108 graduate fields of study. It means a library of more than four million volumes, a faculty of more than 4,300, and a student body of more than 58,000 on six campuses.

It has been said that those who enter a university walk on hallowed ground. And hallowed ground it is at Ohio State. It is where students from all over the world come to learn for the betterment of themselves as individuals and for the betterment of society as a whole. It is where faculty labor long and often solitary hours to test the truth and seek new revelations in almost every area of learning known today. It is where relationships are made among students, faculty, staff, and alumni; relationships that may last a lifetime or be remembered and cherished forever.

The Ohio State University was once just an exciting idea here at the Alumni Association. Now it is a reality, a masterpiece you can hold in your hands. We want this book to *be* Ohio State in the hands and hearts of those who studied here, who lived here, and who now represent The Ohio State University wherever they may be. We also want this book to be a stirring portrait that recalls Ohio State to the minds of its many friends and visitors.

A portrait, defined precisely, is a pictorial representation of a person. We've stretched that definition a little bit, in that Ohio State is not a person per se, but Ohio State has many faces, the most moving and memorable of which we have captured for you in this book.

Ohio State is people — now nearly 87,000 — coming together every day over the years to teach, learn, research, serve, and achieve, or contribute to the administration, operation, and maintenance of the enterprise. We show you some of those people as examples of the timeless whole of Ohio State — a constantly changing, flowing progression of individuals who touch the university, bring it to life, and in turn, are touched and formed by it.

Ohio State has many faces. It is buildings and grounds, statues and equipment, inside and outside. It is summer and winter, fall and spring, night and day. It is sunshine and clouds, rain and snow, knowledge and the seeking of knowledge. It is old and new and all the years in between. It is tradition, it is time and change.

All of it makes up the essence of The Ohio State University. We are delighted to share it all with you once again in this magnificent book.

Dan L. Heinlen
Director of Alumni Affairs
The Ohio State University Alumni Association

Biology and Zoology Building

INTRODUCTION

En route from one appointment to another not long ago, when I was stopped by a traffic light on New York's Madison Avenue, a gentleman touched my arm and said,"You won't remember me, but about ten years ago, you signed my college diploma. I just wanted to say hello, and to tell you what my Alma Mater means to me." And there he stopped, his eyes expressing the difficulty of doing so. There was nothing surprising about either the statements or the unfulfilled wish. My signature is affixed to the degrees of over one-half of all living Ohio State alumni — and I should have equal difficulty in expressing what that awesome fact means to me! Since we both understood that there was no need for either of us to say more, we shook hands warmly, and parted.

In essence, a university is an idea which, through conditioning and modifying and enlarging the sets of values by which people are guided — becomes part of those with whom it comes in contact, and shapes their lives. The proof of its worth are the ways in which those people then live and serve society — in small as well as great ways — the unsung as well as the acclaimed.

Almost no day goes by without our receiving word of another addition to this priceless treasure. For example, a visiting professor speaks gratefully of the invigorating atmosphere and the warm hospitality he has enjoyed. Foreign institutions express appreciation for the benefits from our visiting faculty or staff. The president of Rio Grande College prefaced his praise with a long, detailed list of the many ways in which our school has helped his. Last December a mother and father wrote to tell us that their initial apprehensions about exposing a "country boy" to the "sophisticated teachers" of a cosmopolitan university had vanished.

They concluded a charming letter by labeling themselves "part of the silent majority which appreciates Ohio State's climate conducive to learning within respected boundaries of freedom."

Very few days pass without eloquent words from a perceptive undergraduate or a former student. One was grateful for, as he put it, having been led to the threshhold of his own mind. Another quoted an analogy: "Ohio State is like a mist," he said,"You can't put your finger on it, but you can't be in it very long before you are completely soaked."

Some use symbols in an attempt to pin down the mutual, but elusive, feeling. One young lady explained that the Long Walk at noon on a sunny day *stood* for her Alma Mater; another, that it was represented by Mirror Lake, including the fragrance of its artesian spring! Others select the melodies of Orton Hall Chimes on a crisp, clear October morning.

In such matters, there is no valid reason for uniformity. The important matter is that all looking-back-with-nostalgia is immediately followed by looking ahead with unclouded vision, and dogged integrity. With full acceptance of such a requirement, for justifiable pomp and circumstance, you and The Ohio State University — together — have good reason for what a popular song calls "Walkin' Proud and Happy." We have *every* reason for standing tall! And, from this vantage point, let us spread abroad the message which lies at the heart of cherished campus memories. Help us make the music of the Chimes, with their lilting affirmation of discipline and dedication and effort and hope, part of the universal language of mankind.

Dr. Novice G. Fawcett
President, The Ohio State University

(Reproduced from the Centennial Issue of *The Ohio State University Monthly*, April, 1970)

Ramseyer Hall

T · H · E
OHIO
STATE
UNIVERSITY

An artist creating a portrait of The Ohio State University
would face a difficult task indeed: not only to represent
familiar landmarks, the physical beauty of a campus that
has matured for over a century, but also to try to capture
the spirit, the mood, of the University. Quiet contemplation,
lively debate, the apparent chaos of the search for knowledge
at the frontier, and the meticulous performance of precisely
defined tasks — all would be portrayed.

The spirit of inquiry which permeates the University has
sustained a rich tradition of academic endeavor which we
have inherited — a tradition we nourish and invigorate by
continually challenging and renewing it. This is our common
task. The diversity of people and of methods which go into
this endeavor make Ohio State a truly great university,
whose spirit is reflected in the dedication to excellence
of our students, faculty, and staff members, and in the
loyalty and the lasting achievements of our alumni.

Edward H. Jennings
President, The Ohio State University
February, 1987

After all, a university like ours is not a thing of stones, and bricks and mortar; it is a living thing, a thing of sentiment, a thing that lives in the minds and sentiments of those who have passed through its portals.

Paul M. Lincoln, semicentennial speech, October, 1920

Olentangy River

26

*College years are the closing years of the most
receptive period of life. Let us send out our graduates
into the busy walks of life with the undying memory
of a beautiful university, and with an insatiable
desire to come back every year at Commencement,
with their good classmates, to renew the friendship
of her wide lawns, her shaded walks and her
splendid halls.*

Charles St. John Chubb in *The Ohio State
University Quarterly*, April, 1910

The Outdoor Performance Center at the Browning Ampitheater and Mirror Lake.

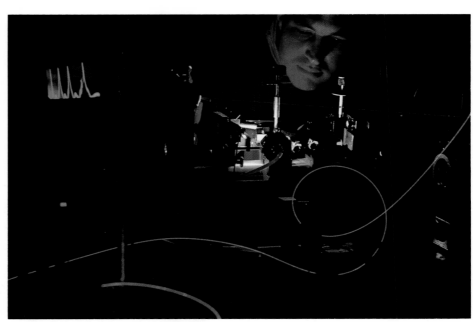

Laserspectroscopy Laboratory

Plant Pathology

The University will be a glory to the state, a light and an inspiration to all who value and seek after the things of the mind.

William H. Scott, ca. 1890

Agronomy Greenhouse

I do not walk down a brick-paved street to my labors; I come into a beautiful green park.
Flowers bloom where I tread in the springtime...I see the colors of the autumn leaves.
I have watched the sunsets (if not the sunrises). There is no more beautiful place
than our campus in all the country.

Professor Billy Graves, Class of 1893

Hayes Hall

(Charles Riley) had talked to a couple of runners I'd become quite close to, Dave Albritton and Ralph Metcalfe, and they were going to Ohio State. But, to be frank, the day I stepped out of Albritton's beat-up car...and first set foot on the campus, I still wasn't convinced.
"Let's see the stadium first," I said. "That's where we'll be running."
The instant I stood inside that stadium, I felt something I'd never felt before. Oh, it was awesome and beautiful — the only place to compare with it would be Berlin's stadium at the '36 Olympics — yet it was something else that took hold of me. I knew I'd win there. I knew I'd break the world's record there.

Jesse Owens

Jesse Owens Memorial

William Oxley Thompson Memorial Library

Universities grow through the creative power of imagination and
the persistent influence of University sentiment and tradition. These
find expression chiefly in the alumni...The future of the University
is largely in the hands of the alumni.

William Oxley Thompson

Orton Hall

Overleaf: Lincoln Tower

51

Do you remember a clear, frosty night when you crossed the cinder path and watched the college lights grow nearer? Our college halls assume an added grandeur, a new poetry by night.

Laura Thomas, in 1909 *The Ohio State University Quarterly*

Last night I couldn't sleep and I wandered around campus in a mood of nostalgia. And there was University Hall, for which I have a kind of terrible affection. Annetta Lu Cornell was one of my classmates. (Her father, incidentally, wrote "Carmen Ohio"). Annetta and I used to smoke between classes, and I have a confession to make after all these years. Annetta and I used to drop matches down the stairwell, hoping to burn down the building. We never succeeded. Future generations — I apologize. I remember also one other thing happened when Annetta and I were smoking between classes. A spinsterish-looking female instructor came up to her when Annetta was puffing away at a cigarette, and with a stony look said to her, "Young lady, I would just as soon be caught in a compromising situation with a strange man as to be caught smoking in public." And without missing a puff, Annetta looked her right in the teeth and said, "So would I, but we only have ten minutes." Memories, memories...

Jerome Lawrence, Commencement, June, 1963

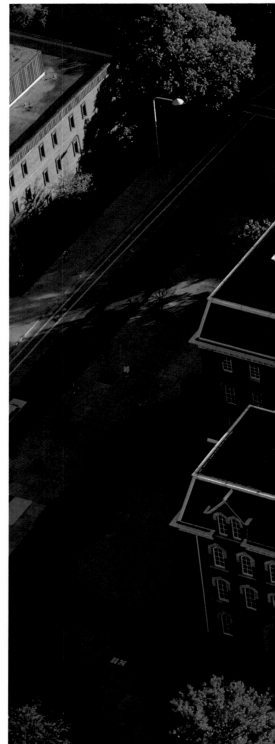

University Hall

French Field House

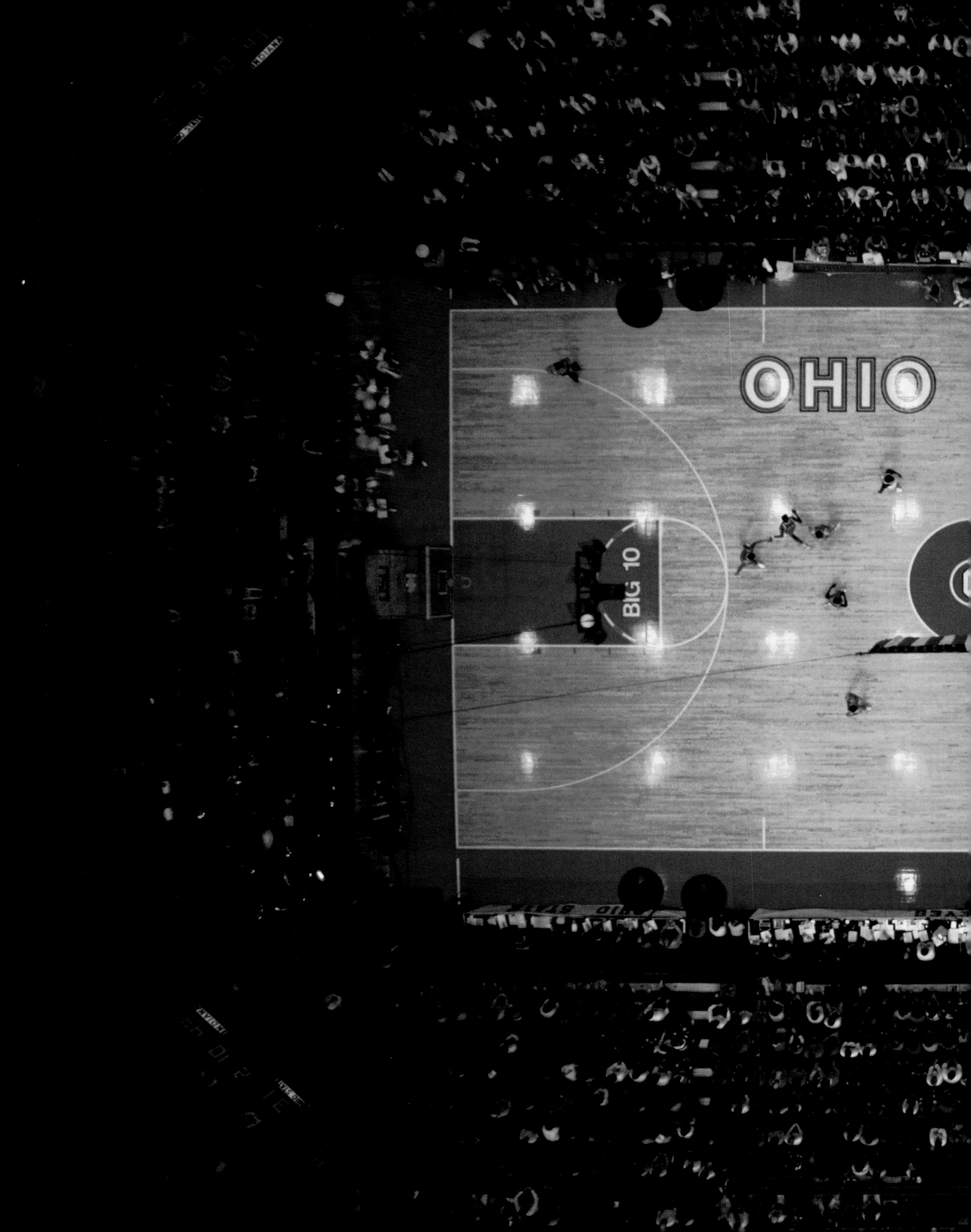
OHIO
BIG 10

Intramural Soccer

Overleaf: Phi Mu Serenade

Homecoming Dance

And about 11:00 at night, when the tired mechanics wanted their best sleep, the fellows would get out in the halls and indulge in their much-needed muscular and vocal gymnastics... At first the profs were unanimous in the opinion that severe penalty should be meted out for such folly, excepting "Prexy" Orton. He said, "Gentlemen, we must make some allowance for young blood."

Frederick W. Sperr, Class of 1883

Sorority Row

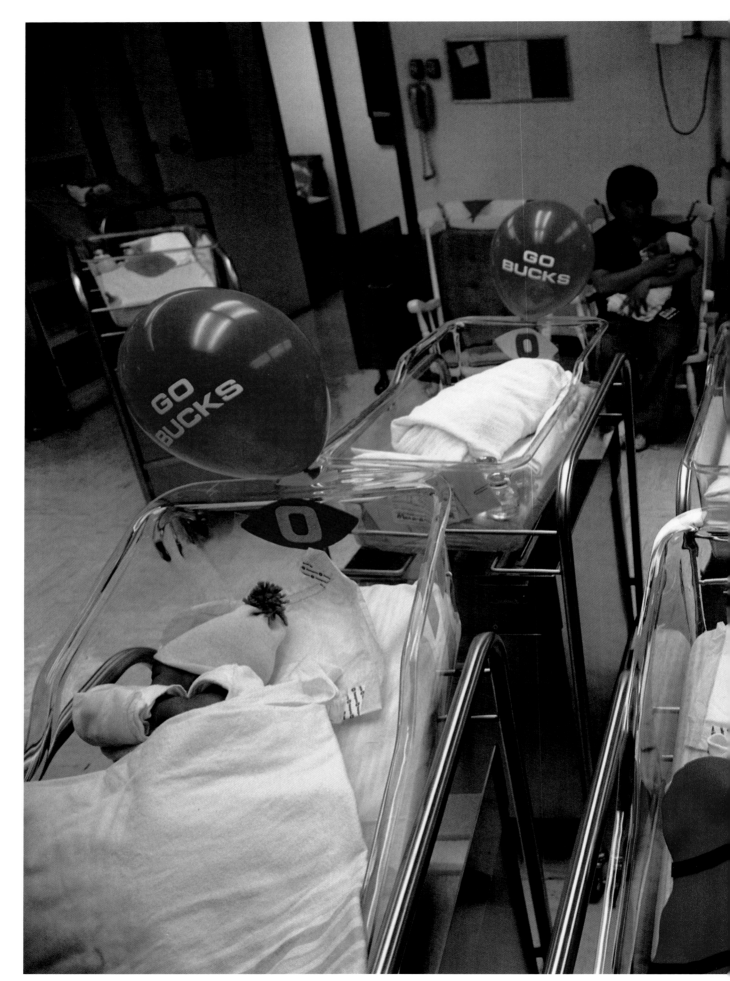

University Hospitals

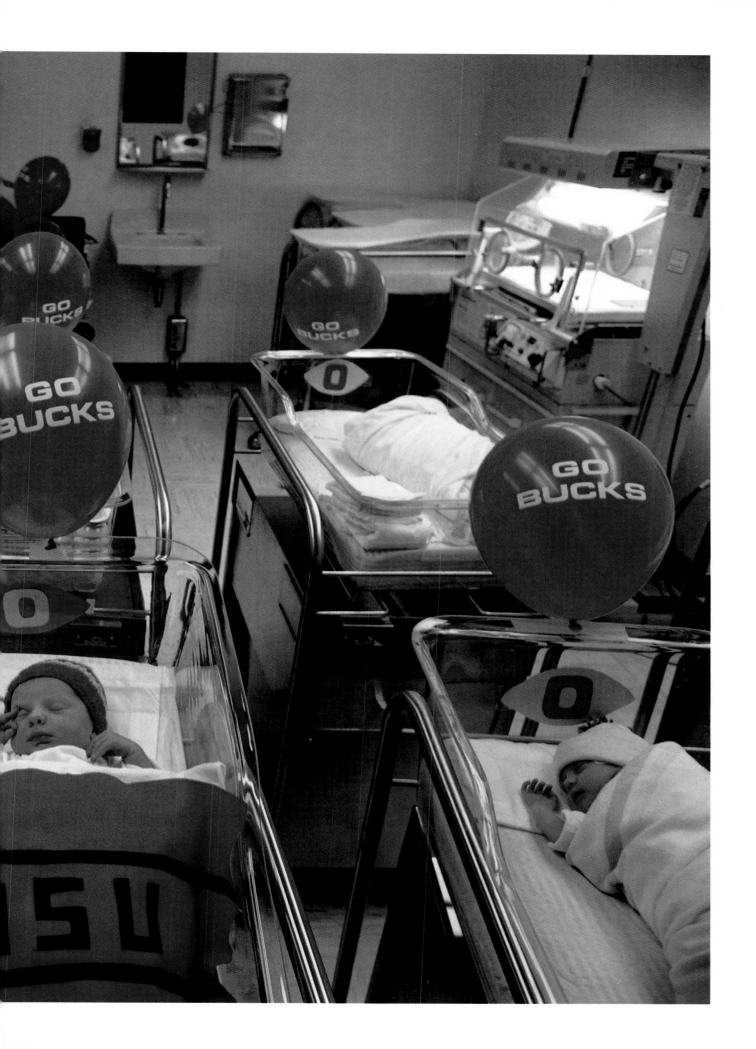

Homecoming Bonfire

Homecoming

It is a very great honor for me to be at The Ohio State University, sometimes known as the Land of the Free and the Home of Woody Hayes. I met Woody at the airport. We just had our picture taken together and when the picture appears in today's Dispatch, I'm pretty sure what the caption will say: Woody Hayes and friend.

President Gerald Ford, Commencement Address, 1974

Department of Black Studies

We can see only a short distance into the future, and it is difficult, if not impossible, to know how the winds of change will affect continued growth and development. But a look at the trends of the past, combined with an analysis of the present, suggests that The Ohio State University will continue to grow in strength and character, will continue to respond to new needs and will continue to make significant contributions to the society it was created to serve.

Dr. Novice G. Fawcett in "The Ringing Grooves of Change," 1970

WOSU Television Control Center

Overleaf: BioScience Electron Microscope

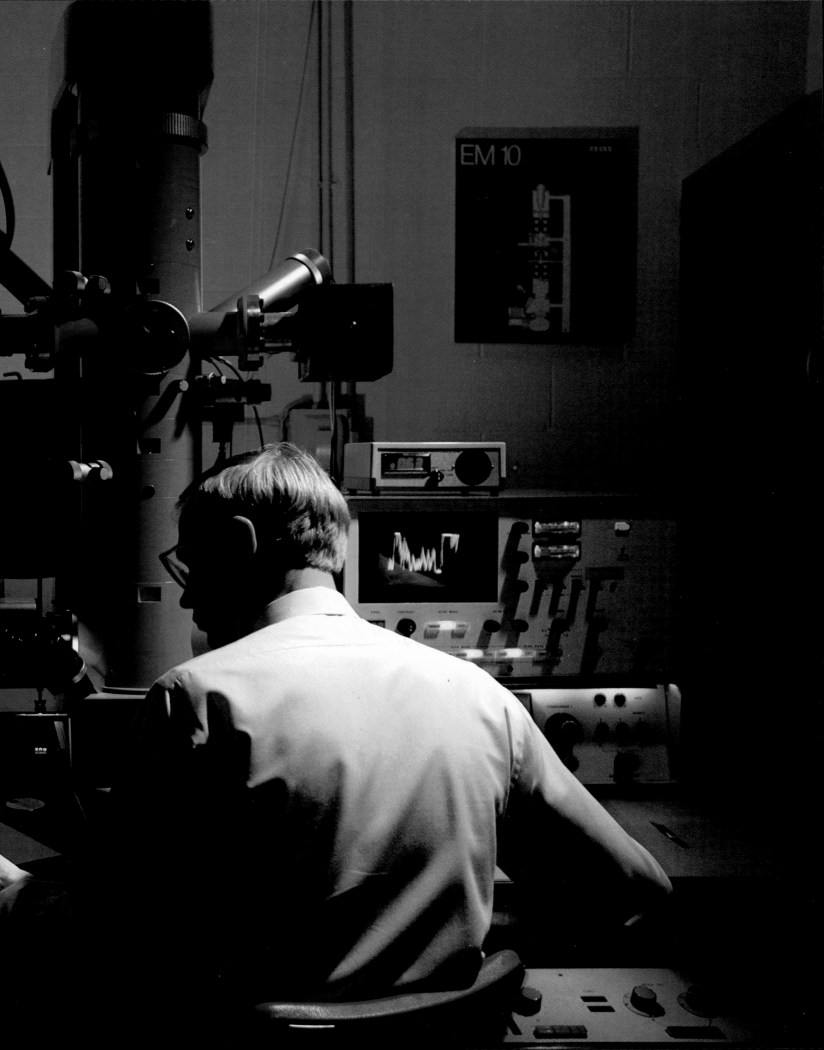

We are justly proud of this beautiful campus, these stately buildings, the library and laboratories...But these things are not the University. The elements of which it is composed are more enduring than stone or steel. It is a thing of power and purpose, of character and influence and inspiration, that manifests itself in the personality of teacher and student-- a community of interests and ideals, endowed by a spirit of sacrifice and devotion on the part of the former, and of loyalty and gratitude on the part of the other, that is to be found in no other relationship.

Lowry F. Sater, in *The Ohio State University Monthly*, 1920

Happily for this University, young ladies were admitted at the beginning upon equal terms with the young men, and experience has justified the policy as being right in every way.

Walter Quincy Scott, ca. 1881

Oh! Come let's sing Ohio's praise,
And songs to Alma Mater raise;
While our heart's rebounding thrill,
With joy which death alone can still.
Summer's heat or Winter's cold,
The seasons pass, the years will roll;
Time and change will surely show
How firm thy friendship--Ohio.

"Carmen Ohio" by Fred A. Cornell '06

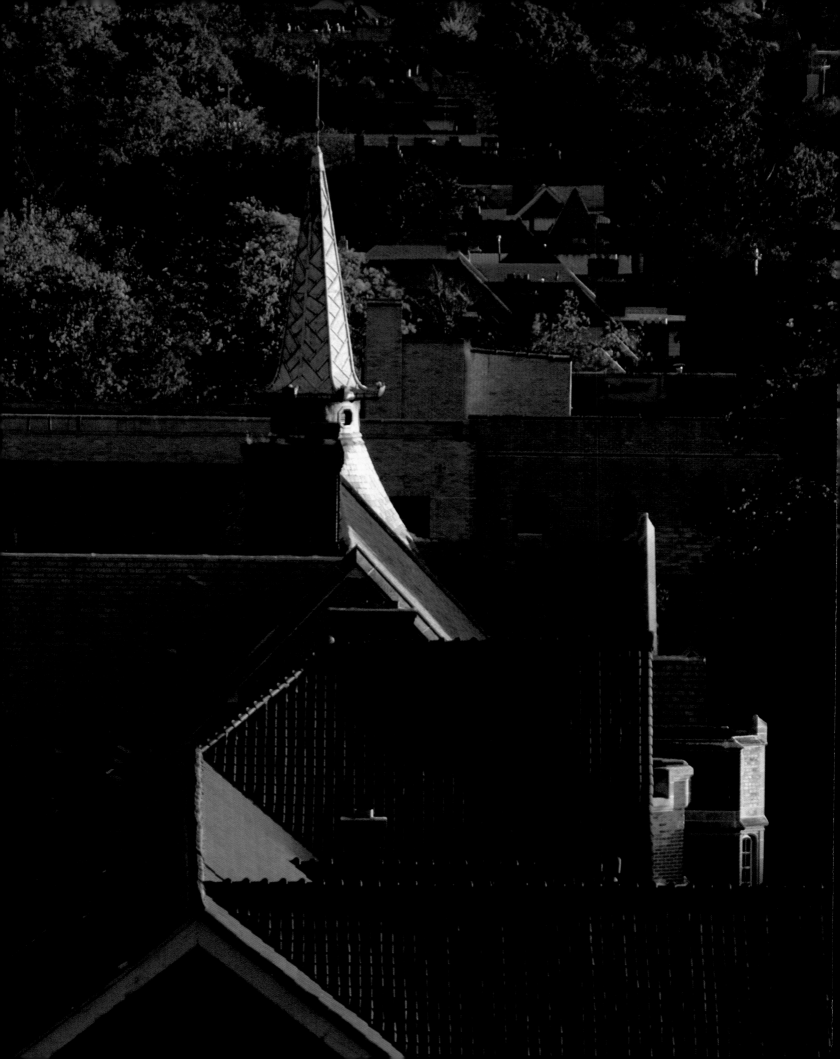

Orton Hall

Mack Hall

Senior, we are sorry to see you go. The others will come back, but not you.
Oh, after a while you will return, married and prosperous, but the college
boy you are now, never— you are saying goodbye to him. But you have a host
of things to carry away with you, and of these, the ideals of the University
itself should mean most to you. Four years she has let you stay beneath her
sheltering roofs and her green trees, and she has given you gladly of all that
is hers of inspiration and great purpose and trustworthy affection. Be grateful,
all of your life. This will not come again. Goodbye, Senior, and God speed you.
And when you've made your mark, come back, again and again. The University
will still be here. She'll always be here.

"The Idler" in *The Lantern*, June, 1906

The great audience was banked around the floor...so that when the caps and gowns nodded and volumed in, and were massed in the center, they were girdled with an unbroken circle of friendly glitter, a happy composition.

The Ohio State University Quarterly, Commencement, 1911

Many years ago, on a hot, summer afternoon, I walked from Derby Hall to the old Ohio Union. Few people were on a then-quiet campus. The campus was green and the sun shone brightly. The campus chimes were dramatically clear and melodious; I had just completed my last final examination. And during that short walk, I became profoundly aware that I would soon be a graduate of one of the world's leading institutions of higher education. Rather than being a moment of extreme elation, it was an especially poignant moment instead. My days on campus were joyous—and I clearly realized that this university had added a new and beneficial dimension to my life. I had a place in The Ohio State University family. From that time on, I have had a strong feeling of closeness, pride and loyalty concerning the University.

Robert M. Duncan , Fall, 1986